50 Holiday Feasts for the Modern Family

By: Kelly Johnson

Table of Contents

- Herb-Crusted Roast Beef
- Honey Glazed Ham
- Baked Turkey with Cranberry Sauce
- Stuffed Pork Tenderloin
- Roast Chicken with Lemon and Thyme
- Grilled Salmon with Garlic Butter
- Vegetable Wellington
- Slow-Cooked Prime Rib
- Braised Short Ribs
- Mushroom and Spinach Lasagna
- Maple-Glazed Carrots
- Sweet Potato Casserole
- Crispy Brussels Sprouts with Balsamic Vinegar
- Garlic Mashed Potatoes
- Mac and Cheese with a Crunchy Topping
- Cranberry-Pecan Salad
- Roasted Butternut Squash Soup
- Green Bean Almondine
- Cornbread Stuffing
- Sautéed Garlic Mushrooms
- Roasted Beet Salad with Goat Cheese
- Grilled Vegetables with Herb Dressing
- Creamed Spinach
- Baked Ziti with Ricotta and Marinara
- Vegetarian Shepherd's Pie
- Holiday Roast Duck with Orange Glaze
- Lobster Tail with Lemon Butter
- Pecan-Crusted Salmon
- Stuffed Acorn Squash with Quinoa and Cranberries
- Spicy Sweet Potato Fries
- Apple and Walnut Salad
- Garlic Parmesan Roasted Cauliflower
- Braised Lamb Shanks
- Roast Beef with Horseradish Cream
- Pumpkin Ravioli in Sage Butter

- Baked Salmon with Dill Cream Sauce
- Spinach and Ricotta Stuffed Shells
- Honey-Glazed Carrots and Parsnips
- Roasted Potato Wedges with Rosemary
- Pasta Primavera
- Pork Belly with Apple Sauce
- Smoked Brisket
- Chickpea and Sweet Potato Stew
- Gingerbread-Stuffed Apples
- Cranberry Orange Bread
- Chocolate Yule Log Cake
- Pumpkin Pie with Cinnamon Whipped Cream
- Apple Cinnamon Cake
- Coconut Cream Pie
- Eggnog Cheesecake

Herb-Crusted Roast Beef

Ingredients:

- 4-5 lb beef roast (such as ribeye or sirloin)
- 3 tablespoons olive oil
- 2 tablespoons fresh rosemary, chopped
- 2 tablespoons fresh thyme, chopped
- 3 cloves garlic, minced
- Salt and pepper, to taste
- 1 tablespoon Dijon mustard (optional)
- 1/2 cup beef broth (for roasting)

Instructions:

1. **Prepare the Beef**:
   Preheat your oven to 450°F (230°C). Pat the beef roast dry with paper towels.
2. **Season the Roast**:
   In a small bowl, mix the olive oil, rosemary, thyme, garlic, salt, and pepper. Rub the mixture all over the beef roast. If desired, spread a thin layer of Dijon mustard on the roast before applying the herb crust.
3. **Roast the Beef**:
   Place the roast on a roasting rack in a roasting pan. Add beef broth to the pan. Roast for 15-20 minutes to sear the outside, then reduce the oven temperature to 350°F (175°C) and cook for an additional 45 minutes to 1 hour, depending on desired doneness. Use a meat thermometer for accuracy (125°F for rare, 135°F for medium-rare, 145°F for medium).
4. **Rest and Serve**:
   Remove the roast from the oven and let it rest for 10 minutes before slicing. Serve with your favorite sides.

Honey Glazed Ham

Ingredients:

- 1 (8-10 lb) bone-in ham
- 1/2 cup honey
- 1/4 cup Dijon mustard
- 1/4 cup brown sugar
- 1/4 cup apple cider vinegar
- 1/2 teaspoon ground cinnamon
- 1/4 teaspoon ground cloves
- Salt and pepper, to taste

Instructions:

1. **Preheat Oven and Prepare Ham**:
   Preheat the oven to 325°F (165°C). Place the ham on a rack in a roasting pan, and score the surface of the ham in a diamond pattern.
2. **Make the Glaze**:
   In a saucepan, combine the honey, mustard, brown sugar, apple cider vinegar, cinnamon, and cloves. Bring to a simmer over medium heat, stirring occasionally. Let the glaze reduce for about 10-15 minutes until it thickens slightly.
3. **Roast the Ham**:
   Brush the ham with the glaze and place it in the oven. Roast for about 1.5 to 2 hours, basting every 20-30 minutes with the glaze, until the ham reaches an internal temperature of 140°F (60°C).
4. **Serve**:
   Let the ham rest for 10 minutes before slicing. Serve with extra glaze on the side.

Baked Turkey with Cranberry Sauce

Ingredients:

- 1 whole turkey (12-14 lbs)
- 1/4 cup olive oil or butter
- 1 tablespoon garlic powder
- 1 tablespoon onion powder
- 1 tablespoon dried thyme
- Salt and pepper, to taste
- 1 cup chicken broth (for roasting)

For the Cranberry Sauce:

- 12 oz fresh cranberries
- 1 cup sugar
- 1/2 cup orange juice
- Zest of 1 orange
- 1/4 teaspoon ground cinnamon

Instructions:

1. **Prepare the Turkey:**
   Preheat the oven to 325°F (165°C). Remove the giblets and pat the turkey dry. Rub the turkey with olive oil or butter, then season with garlic powder, onion powder, thyme, salt, and pepper.
2. **Roast the Turkey:**
   Place the turkey on a roasting rack in a pan. Pour chicken broth into the bottom of the pan. Roast for about 3-4 hours, basting occasionally, until the internal temperature reaches 165°F (74°C) when measured at the thickest part of the thigh.
3. **Make the Cranberry Sauce:**
   In a saucepan, combine cranberries, sugar, orange juice, orange zest, and cinnamon. Bring to a simmer over medium heat. Cook for about 10-15 minutes, stirring occasionally, until the cranberries burst and the sauce thickens. Let cool before serving.
4. **Serve:**
   Let the turkey rest for 20 minutes before carving. Serve with cranberry sauce on the side.

Stuffed Pork Tenderloin

Ingredients:

- 2 pork tenderloins (about 1 lb each)
- 1 cup spinach, sautéed
- 1/2 cup crumbled feta cheese
- 1/4 cup sun-dried tomatoes, chopped
- 1/4 cup breadcrumbs
- 2 tablespoons olive oil
- 1 teaspoon garlic powder
- Salt and pepper, to taste
- Butcher's twine for tying

Instructions:

1. **Prepare the Stuffing:**
   In a bowl, combine the sautéed spinach, feta cheese, sun-dried tomatoes, and breadcrumbs. Season with salt and pepper.
2. **Stuff the Pork:**
   Carefully slice a pocket into the center of each pork tenderloin. Stuff the mixture into each pocket, then tie the tenderloins with butcher's twine to secure the filling.
3. **Sear and Roast:**
   Heat olive oil in a large skillet over medium-high heat. Sear the pork tenderloins for 2-3 minutes on each side. Transfer to a preheated 375°F (190°C) oven and roast for 20-25 minutes, or until the internal temperature reaches 145°F (63°C).
4. **Serve:**
   Let the pork rest for 10 minutes before slicing. Serve with your favorite sides.

Roast Chicken with Lemon and Thyme

Ingredients:

- 1 whole chicken (about 4 lbs)
- 1 lemon, halved
- 1 bunch fresh thyme
- 4 garlic cloves, smashed
- 2 tablespoons olive oil
- Salt and pepper, to taste

Instructions:

1. **Prepare the Chicken:**
   Preheat the oven to 400°F (200°C). Stuff the chicken cavity with lemon halves, thyme, and garlic cloves. Rub the chicken with olive oil and season generously with salt and pepper.
2. **Roast the Chicken:**
   Place the chicken in a roasting pan and roast for 1 hour 15 minutes to 1 hour 30 minutes, or until the internal temperature reaches 165°F (74°C).
3. **Serve:**
   Let the chicken rest for 10 minutes before carving. Serve with roasted vegetables or potatoes.

Grilled Salmon with Garlic Butter

Ingredients:

- 4 salmon fillets
- 2 tablespoons olive oil
- 3 tablespoons butter, melted
- 3 cloves garlic, minced
- 1 tablespoon fresh lemon juice
- Fresh parsley, chopped, for garnish
- Salt and pepper, to taste

Instructions:

1. **Prepare the Salmon**:
   Preheat the grill to medium-high heat. Brush the salmon fillets with olive oil and season with salt and pepper.
2. **Grill the Salmon**:
   Grill the salmon fillets for about 4-6 minutes per side, depending on thickness, until the salmon is cooked through and flakes easily.
3. **Make the Garlic Butter**:
   In a small bowl, combine the melted butter, garlic, and lemon juice. Drizzle over the grilled salmon.
4. **Serve**:
   Garnish with fresh parsley and serve with your favorite side dishes.

Vegetable Wellington

Ingredients:

- 1 sheet puff pastry
- 1 cup mushrooms, finely chopped
- 1 cup spinach, sautéed and drained
- 1/4 cup ricotta cheese
- 1/4 cup grated Parmesan cheese
- 1 tablespoon fresh thyme, chopped
- 1 egg, beaten (for egg wash)
- Salt and pepper, to taste

Instructions:

1. **Prepare the Filling**:
   Sauté the mushrooms in olive oil until soft. Add the spinach and cook until wilted. Remove excess moisture and combine with ricotta cheese, Parmesan, thyme, salt, and pepper.
2. **Assemble the Wellington**:
   Preheat the oven to 375°F (190°C). Lay out the puff pastry sheet on a baking sheet. Spread the vegetable mixture in the center, leaving space on the edges. Fold the pastry over the filling and seal the edges.
3. **Bake**:
   Brush the pastry with the beaten egg. Bake for 25-30 minutes, or until golden and crispy.
4. **Serve**:
   Slice and serve as a main dish or side.

Slow-Cooked Prime Rib

Ingredients:

- 4-6 lb prime rib roast
- 2 tablespoons olive oil
- 3 cloves garlic, minced
- 2 tablespoons fresh rosemary, chopped
- 1 tablespoon fresh thyme, chopped
- Salt and pepper, to taste
- 1 cup beef broth

Instructions:

1. **Prepare the Prime Rib**:
   Season the prime rib roast with olive oil, garlic, rosemary, thyme, salt, and pepper.
2. **Sear the Roast**:
   Heat a large skillet over high heat. Sear the roast on all sides until browned.
3. **Slow-Cook the Roast**:
   Transfer the roast to a slow cooker. Add beef broth and cook on low for 6-8 hours, or until the meat is tender and reaches an internal temperature of 130°F (54°C) for medium-rare.
4. **Serve**:
   Let the roast rest before slicing and serving.

Braised Short Ribs

Ingredients:

- 4-6 bone-in beef short ribs
- 2 tablespoons olive oil
- 1 onion, chopped
- 2 carrots, chopped
- 2 celery stalks, chopped
- 3 cloves garlic, minced
- 2 cups red wine
- 2 cups beef broth
- 1 sprig fresh rosemary
- Salt and pepper, to taste

Instructions:

1. **Brown the Short Ribs**:
   Heat olive oil in a large pot over medium-high heat. Brown the short ribs on all sides, then remove and set aside.
2. **Cook the Vegetables**:
   In the same pot, sauté the onion, carrots, celery, and garlic until softened, about 5 minutes.
3. **Braised the Ribs**:
   Add the wine and broth, scraping up any bits from the bottom of the pot. Return the short ribs to the pot and add rosemary. Bring to a simmer, cover, and cook on low for 2-3 hours, until the ribs are tender.
4. **Serve**:
   Remove the ribs from the sauce and strain the sauce if desired. Serve the short ribs with the sauce.

Mushroom and Spinach Lasagna

Ingredients:

- 9 lasagna noodles (regular or no-boil)
- 2 tablespoons olive oil
- 1 small onion, chopped
- 3 cloves garlic, minced
- 1 lb mushrooms, sliced (button or cremini)
- 4 cups fresh spinach, wilted
- 2 cups ricotta cheese
- 2 cups shredded mozzarella cheese
- 1 cup grated Parmesan cheese
- 1 egg
- 2 cups marinara sauce
- Salt and pepper, to taste
- Fresh basil (optional)

Instructions:

1. **Prepare the Noodles**:
   Cook the lasagna noodles according to package instructions, drain, and set aside. (If using no-boil noodles, skip this step.)
2. **Prepare the Filling**:
   Heat olive oil in a large skillet over medium heat. Add the onion and garlic and cook until softened, about 5 minutes. Add the mushrooms and cook until they release their moisture and become golden brown, about 10 minutes. Stir in the spinach and cook until wilted, about 2 minutes. Remove from heat and let cool slightly.
3. **Assemble the Lasagna**:
   Preheat your oven to 375°F (190°C). In a bowl, mix the ricotta cheese, egg, and half of the Parmesan. Season with salt and pepper. In a 9x13-inch baking dish, spread a thin layer of marinara sauce on the bottom. Add a layer of lasagna noodles, followed by a layer of the ricotta mixture, mushroom-spinach filling, and mozzarella cheese. Repeat the layers until all ingredients are used, finishing with a layer of marinara sauce and mozzarella cheese on top.
4. **Bake**:
   Cover the lasagna with foil and bake for 30 minutes. Remove the foil and bake for another 15 minutes, until the top is golden and bubbly.

5. **Serve**:
   Let the lasagna rest for 10 minutes before slicing. Garnish with fresh basil, if desired.

Maple-Glazed Carrots

Ingredients:

- 1 lb baby carrots (or sliced carrots)
- 2 tablespoons butter
- 1/4 cup maple syrup
- 1/2 teaspoon cinnamon
- Salt and pepper, to taste
- Fresh parsley (optional)

Instructions:

1. **Cook the Carrots**:
   Bring a pot of salted water to a boil. Add the carrots and cook for 8-10 minutes, until tender. Drain and set aside.
2. **Prepare the Glaze**:
   In a large skillet, melt the butter over medium heat. Stir in the maple syrup and cinnamon, and bring to a simmer. Let cook for 2-3 minutes, until the glaze thickens slightly.
3. **Glaze the Carrots**:
   Add the cooked carrots to the skillet and toss to coat in the maple glaze. Cook for an additional 3-5 minutes, until the carrots are heated through and the glaze has thickened.
4. **Serve**:
   Season with salt and pepper, and garnish with fresh parsley, if desired.

Sweet Potato Casserole

Ingredients:

- 4 large sweet potatoes, peeled and cubed
- 1/2 cup milk (or heavy cream)
- 1/4 cup butter
- 1/2 cup brown sugar
- 1 teaspoon vanilla extract
- 1/2 teaspoon ground cinnamon
- 1/4 teaspoon ground nutmeg
- 1/4 teaspoon salt
- 1 cup mini marshmallows (optional)
- 1/2 cup chopped pecans (optional)

Instructions:

1. **Prepare the Sweet Potatoes**:
   Boil the sweet potatoes in salted water until tender, about 15 minutes. Drain and mash with a potato masher or hand mixer.
2. **Make the Filling**:
   Add the milk, butter, brown sugar, vanilla, cinnamon, nutmeg, and salt to the mashed sweet potatoes. Mix until smooth and creamy.
3. **Assemble the Casserole**:
   Preheat the oven to 350°F (175°C). Transfer the sweet potato mixture into a greased baking dish and spread evenly.
4. **Top and Bake**:
   If using, sprinkle mini marshmallows and chopped pecans on top. Bake for 20-25 minutes, or until the top is golden and bubbly.

Crispy Brussels Sprouts with Balsamic Vinegar

Ingredients:

- 1 lb Brussels sprouts, trimmed and halved
- 2 tablespoons olive oil
- Salt and pepper, to taste
- 2 tablespoons balsamic vinegar
- 1 tablespoon honey (optional)

Instructions:

1. **Prepare the Brussels Sprouts**:
   Preheat your oven to 400°F (200°C). Toss the halved Brussels sprouts with olive oil, salt, and pepper.
2. **Roast the Brussels Sprouts**:
   Spread the Brussels sprouts on a baking sheet in a single layer. Roast for 20-25 minutes, flipping halfway through, until crispy and golden brown on the edges.
3. **Finish with Balsamic**:
   Remove from the oven and drizzle with balsamic vinegar and honey, if desired. Toss to coat evenly.
4. **Serve**:
   Serve immediately as a side dish.

Garlic Mashed Potatoes

Ingredients:

- 2 lbs Yukon gold potatoes, peeled and cubed
- 4 cloves garlic, smashed
- 1/2 cup butter
- 1/2 cup milk or heavy cream
- Salt and pepper, to taste
- Fresh parsley (optional)

Instructions:

1. **Boil the Potatoes**:
   Place the potatoes and garlic in a large pot and cover with cold water. Bring to a boil and cook until the potatoes are tender, about 15 minutes. Drain and return to the pot.
2. **Mash the Potatoes**:
   Add the butter and milk (or cream) to the potatoes. Mash until smooth and creamy. Season with salt and pepper.
3. **Serve**:
   Garnish with fresh parsley, if desired, and serve immediately.

Mac and Cheese with a Crunchy Topping

Ingredients:

- 1 lb elbow macaroni
- 2 cups shredded cheddar cheese
- 1 cup shredded mozzarella cheese
- 2 cups whole milk
- 2 tablespoons butter
- 2 tablespoons all-purpose flour
- 1/2 teaspoon mustard powder
- Salt and pepper, to taste
- 1 cup breadcrumbs (for topping)
- 2 tablespoons melted butter (for topping)

Instructions:

1. **Cook the Pasta**:
   Cook the macaroni according to package instructions, drain, and set aside.
2. **Make the Cheese Sauce**:
   In a saucepan, melt butter over medium heat. Stir in flour and mustard powder, and cook for 1-2 minutes. Gradually add the milk, whisking continuously until smooth and thickened. Remove from heat and stir in the shredded cheeses until melted and creamy. Season with salt and pepper.
3. **Combine the Pasta and Sauce**:
   Combine the cooked macaroni with the cheese sauce and mix well. Transfer to a greased baking dish.
4. **Prepare the Topping**:
   Mix the breadcrumbs with the melted butter and sprinkle over the mac and cheese.
5. **Bake**:
   Preheat the oven to 350°F (175°C) and bake the mac and cheese for 20-25 minutes, until bubbly and golden on top.

Cranberry-Pecan Salad

Ingredients:

- 4 cups mixed greens (spinach, arugula, or kale)
- 1/2 cup dried cranberries
- 1/2 cup toasted pecans
- 1/2 cup crumbled goat cheese (optional)
- 1/4 red onion, thinly sliced
- Balsamic vinaigrette dressing

Instructions:

1. **Assemble the Salad**:
   In a large bowl, combine the mixed greens, cranberries, pecans, goat cheese (if using), and red onion.
2. **Dress the Salad**:
   Toss the salad with balsamic vinaigrette dressing to taste.
3. **Serve**:
   Serve immediately as a refreshing side dish.

Roasted Butternut Squash Soup

Ingredients:

- 1 large butternut squash, peeled and cubed
- 2 tablespoons olive oil
- 1 onion, chopped
- 2 carrots, chopped
- 2 cloves garlic, minced
- 4 cups vegetable broth
- 1 teaspoon ground cinnamon
- Salt and pepper, to taste
- 1/2 cup heavy cream (optional)

Instructions:

1. **Roast the Squash**:
   Preheat the oven to 400°F (200°C). Toss the butternut squash cubes with olive oil, salt, and pepper. Spread on a baking sheet and roast for 25-30 minutes, until tender.
2. **Prepare the Soup Base**:
   In a large pot, sauté the onion, carrots, and garlic in olive oil until softened, about 10 minutes.
3. **Make the Soup**:
   Add the roasted butternut squash to the pot along with the vegetable broth and cinnamon. Bring to a simmer and cook for 10 minutes.
4. **Blend the Soup**:
   Use an immersion blender or transfer the soup in batches to a blender and puree until smooth.
5. **Finish the Soup**:
   Stir in heavy cream (if using) and adjust seasoning with salt and pepper.
6. **Serve**:
   Serve the soup hot, garnished with a drizzle of cream or roasted seeds if desired.

Green Bean Almondine

Ingredients:

- 1 lb green beans, trimmed
- 1/4 cup sliced almonds
- 2 tablespoons butter
- 1 tablespoon lemon juice
- Salt and pepper, to taste

Instructions:

1. **Blanch the Green Beans:**
   Bring a pot of salted water to a boil. Add the green beans and cook for 3-4 minutes until bright green and tender-crisp. Drain and set aside.
2. **Toast the Almonds:**
   In a skillet, melt butter over medium heat. Add the sliced almonds and cook until golden brown, about 3 minutes.
3. **Toss and Serve:**
   Add the cooked green beans to the skillet and toss with the butter and toasted almonds. Stir in lemon juice and season with salt and pepper.
4. **Serve:**
   Serve immediately as a side dish.

Cornbread Stuffing

Ingredients:

- 1 large loaf of cornbread (about 4 cups, cubed)
- 1 tablespoon olive oil or butter
- 1 medium onion, diced
- 2 celery stalks, diced
- 2 cloves garlic, minced
- 1 teaspoon dried sage
- 1 teaspoon dried thyme
- 1/2 teaspoon ground black pepper
- 1/4 teaspoon salt
- 2 cups vegetable or chicken broth
- 1/4 cup chopped fresh parsley
- 1 egg, beaten (optional, for binding)

Instructions:

1. **Prepare the Cornbread**:
   Cut the cornbread into cubes and let it dry out slightly on a baking sheet at room temperature for 1-2 hours, or toast in the oven at 300°F (150°C) for about 10 minutes, stirring halfway through.
2. **Sauté Vegetables**:
   In a large skillet, heat the olive oil or butter over medium heat. Add the onion, celery, and garlic, and sauté until softened, about 5-7 minutes.
3. **Mix Stuffing**:
   In a large bowl, combine the cubed cornbread, sautéed vegetables, sage, thyme, salt, pepper, and parsley. Add the broth gradually, stirring to moisten the mixture. If using, add the beaten egg and mix well.
4. **Bake**:
   Transfer the stuffing to a greased baking dish and bake at 350°F (175°C) for 25-30 minutes, until the top is golden brown.

Sautéed Garlic Mushrooms

Ingredients:

- 1 lb mushrooms (button or cremini), sliced
- 3 tablespoons butter
- 2 cloves garlic, minced
- 1 tablespoon fresh parsley, chopped
- Salt and pepper, to taste

Instructions:

1. **Sauté the Mushrooms**:
   In a large skillet, melt butter over medium heat. Add the sliced mushrooms and cook, stirring occasionally, until tender and golden brown, about 7-10 minutes.
2. **Add Garlic**:
   Add the minced garlic and sauté for another 1-2 minutes, until fragrant.
3. **Season and Serve**:
   Season with salt, pepper, and fresh parsley. Serve immediately.

Roasted Beet Salad with Goat Cheese

Ingredients:

- 3 medium beets, peeled and diced
- 2 tablespoons olive oil
- Salt and pepper, to taste
- 4 cups mixed greens (arugula, spinach, etc.)
- 1/4 cup crumbled goat cheese
- 1/4 cup chopped walnuts or pecans (optional)
- 2 tablespoons balsamic vinegar
- 1 tablespoon honey (optional)

Instructions:

1. **Roast the Beets**:
   Preheat the oven to 400°F (200°C). Toss the diced beets with olive oil, salt, and pepper. Spread them out on a baking sheet and roast for 30-35 minutes, or until tender. Let them cool.
2. **Prepare the Salad**:
   In a large bowl, toss the mixed greens with the roasted beets. Add crumbled goat cheese and chopped nuts.
3. **Make Dressing**:
   In a small bowl, whisk together the balsamic vinegar and honey (if using). Drizzle over the salad.
4. **Serve**:
   Toss gently and serve immediately.

Grilled Vegetables with Herb Dressing

Ingredients:

- 1 zucchini, sliced
- 1 yellow squash, sliced
- 1 red bell pepper, cut into strips
- 1 onion, cut into wedges
- 1 tablespoon olive oil
- Salt and pepper, to taste
- 1/4 cup fresh herbs (such as parsley, thyme, and basil), chopped
- 2 tablespoons balsamic vinegar

Instructions:

1. **Prepare the Vegetables**:
   Preheat the grill to medium heat. Toss the sliced zucchini, yellow squash, bell pepper, and onion with olive oil, salt, and pepper.
2. **Grill the Vegetables**:
   Grill the vegetables for 4-5 minutes on each side, until they have nice grill marks and are tender.
3. **Make the Herb Dressing**:
   In a small bowl, combine the fresh herbs and balsamic vinegar.
4. **Serve**:
   Drizzle the herb dressing over the grilled vegetables and serve immediately.

Creamed Spinach

Ingredients:

- 4 cups fresh spinach
- 2 tablespoons butter
- 2 cloves garlic, minced
- 1/4 cup heavy cream
- 1/2 cup grated Parmesan cheese
- Salt and pepper, to taste
- 1/4 teaspoon ground nutmeg (optional)

Instructions:

1. **Wilt the Spinach**:
   In a large skillet, cook the spinach over medium heat until wilted, about 3-4 minutes. Drain any excess liquid and set aside.
2. **Make the Cream Sauce**:
   In the same skillet, melt the butter over medium heat. Add the garlic and cook until fragrant, about 1 minute. Stir in the heavy cream and bring to a simmer.
3. **Finish the Dish**:
   Add the Parmesan cheese, salt, pepper, and nutmeg, and stir until smooth. Add the wilted spinach to the skillet and toss to coat. Cook for an additional 2-3 minutes, until heated through.
4. **Serve**:
   Serve immediately as a creamy side dish.

Baked Ziti with Ricotta and Marinara

Ingredients:

- 1 lb ziti pasta
- 2 cups ricotta cheese
- 2 cups marinara sauce
- 2 cups shredded mozzarella cheese
- 1/2 cup grated Parmesan cheese
- 2 tablespoons chopped fresh basil
- Salt and pepper, to taste

Instructions:

1. **Cook the Pasta**:
   Preheat your oven to 350°F (175°C). Cook the ziti pasta according to package instructions, drain, and set aside.
2. **Combine the Ingredients**:
   In a large bowl, mix the cooked ziti, ricotta cheese, marinara sauce, half of the mozzarella, and Parmesan. Season with salt and pepper.
3. **Assemble the Dish**:
   Transfer the pasta mixture to a greased baking dish. Top with the remaining mozzarella cheese and fresh basil.
4. **Bake**:
   Bake for 25-30 minutes, until bubbly and golden on top.

Vegetarian Shepherd's Pie

Ingredients:

- 4 large potatoes, peeled and cubed
- 2 tablespoons butter
- 1/4 cup milk
- Salt and pepper, to taste
- 1 tablespoon olive oil
- 1 onion, chopped
- 2 carrots, diced
- 1 cup frozen peas
- 1 cup corn kernels
- 2 cups vegetable broth
- 2 tablespoons tomato paste
- 1 tablespoon soy sauce
- 1 tablespoon flour

Instructions:

1. **Make the Mashed Potatoes:**
   Boil the potatoes in salted water until tender, about 15 minutes. Drain and mash with butter, milk, salt, and pepper.
2. **Cook the Vegetables:**
   Heat olive oil in a large skillet over medium heat. Add the onion and carrots and sauté until softened, about 5 minutes. Add peas and corn and cook for another 2-3 minutes.
3. **Make the Filling:**
   Stir in the flour, tomato paste, and soy sauce. Gradually add the vegetable broth, stirring to combine. Cook for another 5 minutes, until the sauce thickens.
4. **Assemble the Pie:**
   Transfer the vegetable mixture to a greased baking dish. Spread the mashed potatoes evenly on top.
5. **Bake:**
   Bake at 375°F (190°C) for 20 minutes, until the top is golden.

Holiday Roast Duck with Orange Glaze

Ingredients:

- 1 whole duck (about 5-6 lbs)
- 1 tablespoon olive oil
- Salt and pepper, to taste
- 2 cups orange juice
- 1/4 cup honey
- 1/4 cup soy sauce
- 1 tablespoon grated ginger
- 1 tablespoon cornstarch (optional for thickening)

Instructions:

1. **Prepare the Duck**:
   Preheat the oven to 350°F (175°C). Rub the duck with olive oil, salt, and pepper. Place it on a roasting rack in a roasting pan.
2. **Roast the Duck**:
   Roast the duck for 1.5-2 hours, basting every 30 minutes with its own juices.
3. **Make the Orange Glaze**:
   In a small saucepan, combine the orange juice, honey, soy sauce, and ginger. Bring to a simmer and cook until reduced by half, about 15 minutes. For a thicker glaze, mix cornstarch with a tablespoon of water and stir into the sauce. Simmer for an additional 2 minutes.
4. **Serve**:
   Drizzle the orange glaze over the roasted duck before serving.

Lobster Tail with Lemon Butter

Ingredients:

- 4 lobster tails
- 1/4 cup butter, melted
- 2 tablespoons fresh lemon juice
- 1 teaspoon garlic powder
- Salt and pepper, to taste
- Fresh parsley, chopped (optional)

Instructions:

1. **Prepare the Lobster Tails**:
   Preheat your oven to 425°F (220°C). Use kitchen scissors to cut the top of the lobster tails down the middle, then gently pull the meat out and lay it on top of the shell.
2. **Make the Butter Sauce**:
   Mix the melted butter with lemon juice, garlic powder, salt, and pepper.
3. **Bake the Lobster Tails**:
   Place the lobster tails on a baking sheet and brush with the lemon butter sauce. Bake for 12-15 minutes, or until the lobster meat is opaque and cooked through.
4. **Serve**:
   Garnish with fresh parsley and serve with additional lemon butter sauce on the side.

Pecan-Crusted Salmon

Ingredients:

- 4 salmon fillets
- 1 cup pecans, finely chopped
- 1/2 cup panko breadcrumbs
- 1 tablespoon Dijon mustard
- 2 tablespoons honey
- 2 tablespoons olive oil
- Salt and pepper, to taste

Instructions:

1. **Prepare the Salmon**:
   Preheat the oven to 375°F (190°C). Place the salmon fillets on a baking sheet lined with parchment paper. Season with salt and pepper.
2. **Make the Crust**:
   In a bowl, mix the chopped pecans, panko breadcrumbs, and honey. Brush each salmon fillet with Dijon mustard, then press the pecan mixture onto the fillets.
3. **Bake**:
   Drizzle olive oil over the crusted salmon and bake for 15-20 minutes, or until the salmon is cooked through and the crust is golden brown.
4. **Serve**:
   Serve the salmon with a drizzle of honey or a squeeze of lemon if desired.

Stuffed Acorn Squash with Quinoa and Cranberries

Ingredients:

- 2 acorn squash, halved and seeded
- 1 cup cooked quinoa
- 1/2 cup dried cranberries
- 1/4 cup chopped walnuts
- 1 tablespoon olive oil
- 1 teaspoon cinnamon
- Salt and pepper, to taste
- 1 tablespoon maple syrup (optional)

Instructions:

1. **Roast the Squash**:
   Preheat the oven to 400°F (200°C). Drizzle the cut sides of the acorn squash with olive oil and season with salt, pepper, and cinnamon. Place the squash halves cut side down on a baking sheet and roast for 25-30 minutes, or until tender.
2. **Prepare the Filling**:
   While the squash is roasting, cook the quinoa according to package instructions. Once cooked, stir in the dried cranberries, chopped walnuts, and maple syrup (if using).
3. **Stuff the Squash**:
   Once the squash halves are roasted and tender, fill the centers with the quinoa mixture. Return to the oven for 10 more minutes to heat through.
4. **Serve**:
   Serve the stuffed acorn squash as a festive side dish.

Spicy Sweet Potato Fries

Ingredients:

- 2 large sweet potatoes, peeled and cut into fries
- 2 tablespoons olive oil
- 1 teaspoon paprika
- 1/2 teaspoon cayenne pepper
- 1/2 teaspoon garlic powder
- Salt and pepper, to taste

Instructions:

1. **Prepare the Fries**:
   Preheat the oven to 425°F (220°C). Toss the sweet potato fries with olive oil, paprika, cayenne, garlic powder, salt, and pepper until well-coated.
2. **Bake**:
   Arrange the fries in a single layer on a baking sheet. Bake for 20-25 minutes, flipping halfway through, until golden and crispy.
3. **Serve**:
   Serve the spicy sweet potato fries with a dipping sauce, such as ranch or a spicy aioli.

Apple and Walnut Salad

Ingredients:

- 4 cups mixed greens (such as arugula, spinach, and kale)
- 2 apples, thinly sliced
- 1/2 cup toasted walnuts
- 1/4 cup crumbled blue cheese or goat cheese (optional)
- 2 tablespoons balsamic vinegar
- 1 tablespoon olive oil
- 1 teaspoon honey
- Salt and pepper, to taste

Instructions:

1. **Make the Dressing**:
   In a small bowl, whisk together the balsamic vinegar, olive oil, honey, salt, and pepper.
2. **Assemble the Salad**:
   In a large bowl, toss the mixed greens with the sliced apples and toasted walnuts. Add the crumbled cheese if using.
3. **Dress the Salad**:
   Drizzle the dressing over the salad and toss gently.
4. **Serve**:
   Serve immediately as a refreshing side dish.

Garlic Parmesan Roasted Cauliflower

Ingredients:

- 1 large head of cauliflower, cut into florets
- 2 tablespoons olive oil
- 3 cloves garlic, minced
- 1/2 cup grated Parmesan cheese
- Salt and pepper, to taste
- 1/4 teaspoon red pepper flakes (optional)
- Fresh parsley, chopped (optional)

Instructions:

1. **Prepare the Cauliflower**:
   Preheat the oven to 400°F (200°C). Toss the cauliflower florets with olive oil, minced garlic, salt, pepper, and red pepper flakes.
2. **Roast the Cauliflower**:
   Spread the cauliflower in a single layer on a baking sheet. Roast for 20-25 minutes, until the cauliflower is tender and slightly browned.
3. **Add Parmesan**:
   Remove the cauliflower from the oven and sprinkle with grated Parmesan. Return to the oven for an additional 5-7 minutes, until the cheese is melted and golden.
4. **Serve**:
   Garnish with chopped parsley and serve as a savory side dish.

Braised Lamb Shanks

Ingredients:

- 4 lamb shanks
- 2 tablespoons olive oil
- Salt and pepper, to taste
- 1 onion, chopped
- 2 carrots, chopped
- 2 cloves garlic, minced
- 1 cup red wine
- 2 cups beef or vegetable broth
- 2 sprigs rosemary
- 2 sprigs thyme

Instructions:

1. **Sear the Lamb**:
   Preheat the oven to 350°F (175°C). Heat olive oil in a large Dutch oven over medium-high heat. Season the lamb shanks with salt and pepper and sear them on all sides until browned, about 8 minutes. Remove the lamb and set aside.
2. **Sauté the Vegetables**:
   In the same pot, add the onion, carrots, and garlic. Sauté for 5-7 minutes until softened.
3. **Deglaze and Braise**:
   Add the red wine and broth, scraping the bottom of the pot to release any browned bits. Return the lamb shanks to the pot and add the rosemary and thyme. Cover and place in the oven. Braise for 2-2.5 hours, until the lamb is tender.
4. **Serve**:
   Serve the lamb shanks with the braised vegetables and sauce.

Roast Beef with Horseradish Cream

Ingredients:

- 1 (4-5 lb) boneless beef roast (such as rib-eye or sirloin)
- 2 tablespoons olive oil
- Salt and pepper, to taste
- 2 cloves garlic, minced
- 2 tablespoons fresh rosemary, chopped
- 1 cup heavy cream
- 2 tablespoons prepared horseradish
- 1 teaspoon lemon juice

Instructions:

1. **Roast the Beef:**
   Preheat the oven to 400°F (200°C). Rub the beef roast with olive oil, minced garlic, rosemary, salt, and pepper. Place the roast on a roasting rack and roast for 50-60 minutes, or until the internal temperature reaches 135°F (medium-rare).
2. **Make the Horseradish Cream:**
   While the beef is roasting, whip the heavy cream until stiff peaks form. Gently fold in the horseradish and lemon juice. Season with salt to taste.
3. **Rest the Roast:**
   Remove the roast from the oven and let it rest for 10 minutes before slicing.
4. **Serve:**
   Serve the roast beef slices with a dollop of horseradish cream.

Pumpkin Ravioli in Sage Butter

Ingredients:

- 12-16 pumpkin ravioli (store-bought or homemade)
- 4 tablespoons butter
- 8 fresh sage leaves
- Salt and pepper, to taste
- Grated Parmesan cheese, for garnish

Instructions:

1. **Cook the Ravioli**:
   Bring a large pot of salted water to a boil. Cook the pumpkin ravioli according to the package instructions, usually about 3-4 minutes.
2. **Make the Sage Butter**:
   In a large skillet, melt the butter over medium heat. Add the sage leaves and cook for 2-3 minutes until the butter turns golden and fragrant.
3. **Toss the Ravioli**:
   Once the ravioli are cooked, use a slotted spoon to transfer them to the skillet with the sage butter. Gently toss to coat.
4. **Serve**:
   Serve the ravioli with a sprinkle of Parmesan cheese.

Baked Salmon with Dill Cream Sauce

Ingredients:

- 4 salmon fillets
- 1 tablespoon olive oil
- Salt and pepper, to taste
- 1/2 cup sour cream
- 1/4 cup mayonnaise
- 2 tablespoons fresh dill, chopped
- 1 tablespoon lemon juice
- 1 teaspoon Dijon mustard

Instructions:

1. **Prepare the Salmon**:
   Preheat the oven to 375°F (190°C). Place the salmon fillets on a baking sheet lined with parchment paper. Drizzle with olive oil and season with salt and pepper. Bake for 12-15 minutes, or until cooked through.
2. **Make the Dill Cream Sauce**:
   In a small bowl, combine the sour cream, mayonnaise, dill, lemon juice, and Dijon mustard. Stir until smooth.
3. **Serve**:
   Serve the baked salmon fillets with a generous dollop of dill cream sauce on top.

Spinach and Ricotta Stuffed Shells

Ingredients:

- 12 jumbo pasta shells
- 2 cups ricotta cheese
- 2 cups fresh spinach, chopped
- 1/2 cup mozzarella cheese, shredded
- 1/4 cup grated Parmesan cheese
- 1 egg
- 2 cups marinara sauce
- Salt and pepper, to taste
- Fresh basil (optional)

Instructions:

1. **Cook the Pasta**:
   Preheat the oven to 375°F (190°C). Cook the jumbo shells according to package directions, drain, and set aside.
2. **Make the Filling**:
   In a large bowl, combine the ricotta cheese, chopped spinach, mozzarella, Parmesan, egg, salt, and pepper. Mix until well combined.
3. **Stuff the Shells**:
   Carefully stuff each pasta shell with the ricotta and spinach mixture. Place the stuffed shells in a baking dish, seam-side down.
4. **Bake**:
   Pour marinara sauce over the stuffed shells. Cover with foil and bake for 25 minutes. Remove the foil and bake for an additional 5 minutes until the cheese is bubbly.
5. **Serve**:
   Garnish with fresh basil, if desired, and serve hot.

Honey-Glazed Carrots and Parsnips

Ingredients:

- 4 carrots, peeled and cut into sticks
- 4 parsnips, peeled and cut into sticks
- 2 tablespoons honey
- 2 tablespoons olive oil
- 1 teaspoon thyme (fresh or dried)
- Salt and pepper, to taste

Instructions:

1. **Prepare the Vegetables:**
   Preheat the oven to 400°F (200°C). Arrange the carrot and parsnip sticks on a baking sheet.
2. **Make the Glaze:**
   In a small bowl, mix the honey, olive oil, thyme, salt, and pepper.
3. **Roast:**
   Drizzle the honey glaze over the vegetables and toss to coat evenly. Roast for 25-30 minutes, turning halfway through, until the vegetables are tender and caramelized.
4. **Serve:**
   Serve hot as a sweet and savory side dish.

Roasted Potato Wedges with Rosemary

Ingredients:

- 4 large potatoes, cut into wedges
- 2 tablespoons olive oil
- 2 teaspoons fresh rosemary, chopped (or 1 teaspoon dried)
- Salt and pepper, to taste
- 1 garlic clove, minced (optional)

Instructions:

1. **Preheat the Oven**:
   Preheat your oven to 425°F (220°C). Line a baking sheet with parchment paper.
2. **Prepare the Potatoes**:
   Toss the potato wedges with olive oil, rosemary, garlic, salt, and pepper until evenly coated.
3. **Roast**:
   Spread the potato wedges in a single layer on the baking sheet. Roast for 30-35 minutes, flipping once halfway through, until golden and crispy.
4. **Serve**:
   Serve warm as a flavorful side dish.

Pasta Primavera

Ingredients:

- 8 oz pasta (such as spaghetti or penne)
- 2 tablespoons olive oil
- 1 zucchini, sliced
- 1 bell pepper, sliced
- 1 cup cherry tomatoes, halved
- 1/2 cup fresh peas (or frozen)
- 2 cloves garlic, minced
- 1/2 cup Parmesan cheese, grated
- Salt and pepper, to taste
- Fresh basil or parsley for garnish

Instructions:

1. **Cook the Pasta**:
   Cook the pasta according to package directions. Drain, reserving 1/2 cup of pasta water.
2. **Sauté the Vegetables**:
   While the pasta cooks, heat olive oil in a large skillet over medium heat. Add the zucchini, bell pepper, tomatoes, and peas. Sauté for 5-7 minutes until tender.
3. **Combine**:
   Add the cooked pasta and garlic to the skillet with the vegetables. Toss everything together, adding the reserved pasta water to loosen the mixture. Stir in Parmesan cheese and season with salt and pepper.
4. **Serve**:
   Garnish with fresh basil or parsley and serve immediately.

Pork Belly with Apple Sauce

Ingredients:

- 2 lb pork belly, skin scored
- 2 tablespoons olive oil
- Salt and pepper, to taste
- 1 tablespoon fennel seeds (optional)
- 2 apples, peeled, cored, and sliced
- 1/4 cup apple cider vinegar
- 1 tablespoon sugar
- 1/2 teaspoon cinnamon

Instructions:

1. **Prepare the Pork Belly**:
   Preheat the oven to 400°F (200°C). Rub the pork belly with olive oil, salt, pepper, and fennel seeds (if using). Place the pork belly in a roasting pan, skin side up.
2. **Roast the Pork Belly**:
   Roast for 30 minutes at 400°F, then reduce the temperature to 350°F (175°C) and continue roasting for an additional 1.5 hours, until the skin is crispy and the meat is tender.
3. **Make the Apple Sauce**:
   While the pork roasts, cook the apples with cider vinegar, sugar, and cinnamon in a saucepan over medium heat for 15-20 minutes, until the apples break down into a chunky sauce.
4. **Serve**:
   Serve the crispy pork belly with a spoonful of apple sauce on the side.

Smoked Brisket

Ingredients:

- 5-6 lb beef brisket
- 2 tablespoons olive oil
- 1/4 cup smoked paprika
- 2 tablespoons brown sugar
- 1 tablespoon black pepper
- 1 tablespoon salt
- 2 teaspoons garlic powder
- 1 teaspoon onion powder
- 1 teaspoon cumin
- 1/2 cup beef broth

Instructions:

1. **Prepare the Brisket**:
   Preheat your smoker to 225°F (107°C). Rub the brisket with olive oil and coat evenly with a dry rub made from paprika, brown sugar, black pepper, salt, garlic powder, onion powder, and cumin.
2. **Smoke the Brisket**:
   Place the brisket in the smoker and cook for 6-8 hours, or until it reaches an internal temperature of 195°F (90°C).
3. **Rest and Slice**:
   Remove the brisket from the smoker and let it rest for at least 30 minutes before slicing against the grain.
4. **Serve**:
   Serve with your favorite barbecue sauce or on its own.

Chickpea and Sweet Potato Stew

Ingredients:

- 1 tablespoon olive oil
- 1 onion, chopped
- 2 garlic cloves, minced
- 2 sweet potatoes, peeled and cubed
- 1 can chickpeas, drained and rinsed
- 1 can diced tomatoes
- 4 cups vegetable broth
- 1 teaspoon cumin
- 1/2 teaspoon turmeric
- 1 teaspoon cinnamon
- Salt and pepper, to taste
- Fresh cilantro for garnish

Instructions:

1. **Sauté the Vegetables**:
   Heat olive oil in a large pot over medium heat. Add the onion and garlic, cooking for 5 minutes until softened.
2. **Add the Ingredients**:
   Add the sweet potatoes, chickpeas, diced tomatoes, vegetable broth, cumin, turmeric, cinnamon, salt, and pepper. Bring to a boil.
3. **Simmer**:
   Reduce the heat to low and simmer for 30-35 minutes, until the sweet potatoes are tender and the stew has thickened.
4. **Serve**:
   Garnish with fresh cilantro and serve hot.

Gingerbread-Stuffed Apples

Ingredients:

- 4 large apples, cored
- 1/2 cup gingerbread cookie crumbs
- 2 tablespoons butter, melted
- 1 tablespoon brown sugar
- 1/2 teaspoon ground cinnamon
- 1/4 teaspoon ground ginger
- 1/4 teaspoon ground nutmeg
- 1/4 cup chopped walnuts or pecans (optional)
- Whipped cream or vanilla ice cream for serving

Instructions:

1. **Prepare the Apples**:
   Preheat the oven to 375°F (190°C). Place the cored apples in a baking dish.
2. **Make the Filling**:
   In a bowl, combine the gingerbread crumbs, melted butter, brown sugar, cinnamon, ginger, nutmeg, and chopped nuts. Stuff the apples with the gingerbread mixture.
3. **Bake the Apples**:
   Cover the baking dish with foil and bake for 30-40 minutes, until the apples are tender.
4. **Serve**:
   Serve the stuffed apples warm with whipped cream or a scoop of vanilla ice cream.

Cranberry Orange Bread

Ingredients:

- 2 cups all-purpose flour
- 1 1/2 teaspoons baking powder
- 1/2 teaspoon baking soda
- 1/2 teaspoon salt
- 1 teaspoon orange zest
- 1 cup fresh cranberries (or frozen)
- 1/2 cup granulated sugar
- 1/4 cup orange juice
- 2 large eggs
- 1/2 cup unsalted butter, melted
- 1 teaspoon vanilla extract
- 1/2 cup buttermilk

Instructions:

1. **Preheat the Oven:**
   Preheat your oven to 350°F (175°C). Grease and flour a 9x5-inch loaf pan.
2. **Prepare the Dry Ingredients:**
   In a medium bowl, whisk together the flour, baking powder, baking soda, salt, and orange zest.
3. **Prepare the Wet Ingredients:**
   In another bowl, mix the sugar, orange juice, eggs, melted butter, vanilla extract, and buttermilk.
4. **Combine:**
   Add the wet ingredients to the dry ingredients and stir until just combined. Gently fold in the cranberries.
5. **Bake:**
   Pour the batter into the prepared loaf pan. Bake for 50-60 minutes, or until a toothpick inserted in the center comes out clean.
6. **Cool and Serve:**
   Allow the bread to cool in the pan for 10 minutes, then transfer to a wire rack to cool completely before slicing and serving.

Chocolate Yule Log Cake

Ingredients for the Cake:

- 1/2 cup all-purpose flour
- 1/4 cup unsweetened cocoa powder
- 1 teaspoon baking powder
- 1/4 teaspoon salt
- 4 large eggs
- 1 cup granulated sugar
- 1 teaspoon vanilla extract
- 1/4 cup water

Ingredients for the Filling:

- 1 cup heavy cream
- 2 tablespoons powdered sugar
- 1 teaspoon vanilla extract

Ingredients for the Chocolate Frosting:

- 1/2 cup unsalted butter, softened
- 2 cups powdered sugar
- 1/4 cup unsweetened cocoa powder
- 1/4 cup heavy cream
- 1 teaspoon vanilla extract

Instructions:

1. **Prepare the Cake**:
   Preheat the oven to 350°F (175°C). Line a 15x10-inch baking sheet with parchment paper. In a bowl, sift together the flour, cocoa powder, baking powder, and salt.
2. **Make the Cake Batter**:
   In another bowl, beat the eggs and sugar until light and fluffy. Stir in the vanilla extract and water. Gradually fold in the dry ingredients until just combined.
3. **Bake the Cake**:
   Spread the batter evenly on the prepared baking sheet. Bake for 12-15 minutes or until the cake is set. Immediately remove from the oven and roll it up in the parchment paper to cool (this prevents cracking).

4. **Prepare the Filling**:
   Whip the heavy cream, powdered sugar, and vanilla extract until stiff peaks form. Once the cake has cooled, unroll it, spread the whipped cream evenly inside, then roll it back up.
5. **Make the Frosting**:
   Beat the softened butter, powdered sugar, cocoa powder, heavy cream, and vanilla until smooth. Frost the entire cake with the chocolate frosting, creating a "bark" effect with a fork.
6. **Serve**:
   Garnish with powdered sugar or small decorations to resemble holly, then slice and serve!

Pumpkin Pie with Cinnamon Whipped Cream

Ingredients for the Pie:

- 1 pie crust (store-bought or homemade)
- 2 cups pumpkin puree
- 1 cup heavy cream
- 2 large eggs
- 3/4 cup granulated sugar
- 1 teaspoon ground cinnamon
- 1/2 teaspoon ground ginger
- 1/4 teaspoon ground nutmeg
- 1/4 teaspoon ground cloves
- 1/2 teaspoon salt

Ingredients for the Cinnamon Whipped Cream:

- 1 cup heavy cream
- 2 tablespoons powdered sugar
- 1/2 teaspoon ground cinnamon

Instructions:

1. **Preheat the Oven**:
   Preheat the oven to 425°F (220°C).
2. **Prepare the Filling**:
   In a bowl, whisk together the pumpkin puree, heavy cream, eggs, sugar, cinnamon, ginger, nutmeg, cloves, and salt until smooth.
3. **Assemble the Pie**:
   Pour the pumpkin filling into the pie crust. Bake for 15 minutes, then reduce the temperature to 350°F (175°C) and bake for another 45 minutes, or until the center is set.
4. **Make the Whipped Cream**:
   While the pie cools, beat the heavy cream, powdered sugar, and cinnamon until soft peaks form.
5. **Serve**:
   Serve the pie with a dollop of cinnamon whipped cream on top.

Apple Cinnamon Cake

Ingredients:

- 2 cups all-purpose flour
- 1 teaspoon baking powder
- 1 teaspoon ground cinnamon
- 1/2 teaspoon baking soda
- 1/4 teaspoon salt
- 1/2 cup unsalted butter, softened
- 1 cup granulated sugar
- 2 large eggs
- 1 teaspoon vanilla extract
- 1 cup sour cream
- 2 cups peeled, chopped apples (about 2 medium apples)

Instructions:

1. **Preheat the Oven**:
   Preheat the oven to 350°F (175°C). Grease and flour a 9-inch round cake pan.
2. **Mix Dry Ingredients**:
   In a bowl, whisk together the flour, baking powder, cinnamon, baking soda, and salt.
3. **Prepare the Batter**:
   In a separate bowl, beat the butter and sugar until light and fluffy. Add the eggs, one at a time, and vanilla extract. Alternate adding the dry ingredients and sour cream, mixing until combined. Fold in the chopped apples.
4. **Bake the Cake**:
   Pour the batter into the prepared cake pan. Bake for 35-40 minutes, or until a toothpick comes out clean.
5. **Serve**:
   Allow the cake to cool before serving. Optionally, dust with powdered sugar.

Coconut Cream Pie

Ingredients for the Pie Crust:

- 1 1/2 cups graham cracker crumbs
- 1/4 cup granulated sugar
- 1/2 cup unsalted butter, melted

Ingredients for the Filling:

- 1 can (14 oz) coconut milk
- 1 cup whole milk
- 1 cup heavy cream
- 3/4 cup granulated sugar
- 3 tablespoons cornstarch
- 1/2 teaspoon vanilla extract
- 1 cup sweetened shredded coconut

Ingredients for the Topping:

- 1 cup heavy cream
- 2 tablespoons powdered sugar
- 1/2 teaspoon vanilla extract

Instructions:

1. **Make the Pie Crust**:
   Preheat the oven to 350°F (175°C). Mix the graham cracker crumbs, sugar, and melted butter in a bowl. Press the mixture into the bottom of a pie pan. Bake for 10 minutes, then allow to cool.
2. **Prepare the Filling**:
   In a saucepan, combine the coconut milk, whole milk, heavy cream, sugar, and cornstarch. Cook over medium heat, whisking constantly, until the mixture thickens. Stir in the vanilla extract and shredded coconut.
3. **Assemble the Pie**:
   Pour the filling into the cooled crust and refrigerate for at least 4 hours to set.
4. **Make the Whipped Cream Topping**:
   Beat the heavy cream, powdered sugar, and vanilla extract until stiff peaks form. Spread the whipped cream over the pie.
5. **Serve**:
   Serve chilled, garnished with extra shredded coconut, if desired.

Eggnog Cheesecake

Ingredients for the Crust:

- 1 1/2 cups graham cracker crumbs
- 1/4 cup granulated sugar
- 1/2 cup unsalted butter, melted

Ingredients for the Filling:

- 3 (8 oz) packages cream cheese, softened
- 1 cup granulated sugar
- 3 large eggs
- 1/2 cup eggnog
- 1 teaspoon vanilla extract
- 1/4 teaspoon ground nutmeg
- 1/4 teaspoon ground cinnamon

Instructions:

1. **Make the Crust**:
   Preheat the oven to 325°F (160°C). Combine the graham cracker crumbs, sugar, and melted butter in a bowl. Press the mixture into the bottom of a springform pan. Bake for 10 minutes, then cool.
2. **Prepare the Filling**:
   In a bowl, beat the cream cheese and sugar until smooth. Add the eggs one at a time, beating well after each addition. Mix in the eggnog, vanilla extract, nutmeg, and cinnamon.
3. **Bake the Cheesecake**:
   Pour the cheesecake filling into the cooled crust. Bake for 55-60 minutes, or until the center is just set. Turn off the oven and let the cheesecake cool for 1 hour in the oven with the door slightly ajar.
4. **Chill**:
   Refrigerate the cheesecake for at least 4 hours or overnight before serving.
5. **Serve**:
   Garnish with a dusting of nutmeg and serve chilled.